We Became Summer

Also by Amy Barone

Kamikaze Dance, Finishing Line Press (2015)

Views from the Driveway, Foothills Publishing (2008)

We Became Summer

Amy Barone

Books™

The New York Quarterly Foundation, Inc.
New York, New York

NYQ Books™ is an imprint of The New York Quarterly Foundation, Inc.

The New York Quarterly Foundation, Inc.
P. O. Box 2015
Old Chelsea Station
New York, NY 10113

www.nyq.org

First Edition

Set in New Baskerville

Layout by Raymond P. Hammond

Cover Design by Amy Barone and Raymond P. Hammond

Cover Photo by Amy Barone

Author Photo by Blair Hopkins

Library of Congress Control Number: 2018930050

ISBN: 978-1-63045-053-3

For my everyday heroes:
Patrice Adcroft, Ron Kolm, Linda Paskewitz,
and the late Nicholas Novelli

ACKNOWLEDGEMENTS

The author gratefully acknowledges the editors of the following publications where these poems appeared or are forthcoming:

ADANNA
  "Last Words"

Autumn Sky Poetry Daily
  "We Became Summer"

Bentlily.com
  "Views from the Driveway"

Brevitas Anthology
  "Festa Della Donna," "Last Words," "Orange Is My New Black,"
  "Poetry on Demand," "Protected," "Remembered Dreams,"
  "Yellow"

Brownstone Poets Anthology
  "Magazine Street"

Chelsea News
  "A Bridge to Antonio," "Swinging Jazz"

Café Review
  "Bop Juice"

First Literary Review-East
  "Natural Blonde," "Seasonal Nectar"

Gradiva
  "Dreamscapes"

Home Planet News
  "Blank Page," "Chrysalis," "Gold Mine," "Magazine Street,"

"Nineteenth and Sansom," "Power in a Thumb," "Remembered Dreams," "Retro Rider," "Soundtrack to My Life," "Summer Haze," "Venice Reveries"

Impolite Conversation (UK)
"Echoes of a Hardware Store," "Men of the Cloth," "Romance Chelsea Style," "When in Italy," "Yellow"

Italian Americana
"We Became Summer"

Levure Litteraire
"Amelia," "Bahia Beats," "City on a River," "Fashion Monk," "*Festa Della Donna*"

Mediterranean Poetry
"When in Italy"

Möbius, The Poetry Magazine
"At the Bird Sanctuary"

Paterson Literary Review
"Amelia," "Safety"

Philadelphia Poets
"A Bridge to Antonio," "Echoes of a Hardware Store," "Fall in Philadelphia," "Healing Poetry," "Lessons Learned from Moths," "Men of the Cloth," "Nineteenth and Sansom," "Paper Boy's Daughter," "Recollection," "Soundtrack to My Mother's Life," "Soundtrack to My Father's Life," "Travels with You," "Venice Reveries," "When in Italy"

Pink Chameleon
"Contemplating Abruzzo"

Rutherford Red Wheelbarrow
"Clifford Plays Somethin'," "Music Lessons," "Night Revelations," "Passion Sunday," "Power in a Thumb," "Romance Chelsea Style," "Swinging Jazz," "Visions"

Sensitive Skin
"Passion Sunday"

Standpoint (UK)
"End of the Road," "Lessons Learned from Moths," "Master Plan," "Paper Boy's Daughter," "Soundtrack to My Father's Life"

Wild Violet
"Fall in Philadelphia," "Secrets"

Thank you to NYQ Books for the publishing opportunity and for your contribution to the world of poetry. A huge thank you to my literary boosters—Patricia Carragon, Gil Fagiani, Cindy Hochman, Maria Lisella, Karen Neuberg, Angelo Verga, and Alan Wherry. Many thanks to members of the brevitas online poetry community and PEN America Center for supporting my literary work and providing a canvas.

Contents

SOUNDS

HOME

BREEZE

We Became Summer

HEAT

Safety

Safety doesn't come in numbers.
Safety can be found in a single window,
framed with stark white sheers and outside
large granite stones, where happy families must live.

I once found safety in a Joseph Heller book called
Something Happened and grasped why
my English teacher mother had always plagued us
to line our homes with books.

That same day, I found solace in a quart of beer
on a beach in *San Felice Circeo* near Rome, abandoned
by Italian cousins who didn't feel I was family enough.

I often found safety on the driveway as I sat perched
on my purple stingray, cycling in circles watching the world,
especially handsome males, unwittingly writing poetry.

Poetry on Demand

In his innocence
he asks me to write poems
supplies the titles.

How could he understand
the test of mining tales
from the soul?

Reliving death and resurrection,
camouflaging mendacity,
unmasking loved ones?

I doubt I ever possessed
my nephew's purity
at the tender age of six.

Chrysalis

Burrowed in a kitchen corner
a fit lair for a lioness

steaming *espresso macchiato*
in one hand, pen in other,

I start the day in contemplation,
with blue and white tiles as backdrop,

writing on remnants of the unwanted,
the wanted, the reasons I return.

Seasonal Nectar

Plums, with their sweet juicy flesh, stoked desire.
More accessible than forbidden figs whose naked trees
bordered our backyard.

Watermelon signaled a party with cousins or neighbors,
fun and games. Contests where we shot the black seeds
from our mouths, salvaged remains to plant later.

We needed little else.
Warmed ourselves chilly nights dreaming
of ruby fruit that streaked summer days.

Soundtrack to My Life

My soundtrack goes back, ahead, up, down.
"I Saw the Light" as a four-year-old and
got hooked on the British invasion,

pre-Beatles mania. "Maybe I'm Amazed"
by the sheer magic music shed on a
timid child imprisoned in a confused household.

"Ah Mary," my mother—how I adored her
till she wouldn't let me. I finally learned
to smile once I escaped. "What's Going On?"

I make homes wherever I lay my bag.
"I Got a Line on You," New York, no longer him.
It's place that brings me to climax.

Passion Sunday

Furtively, I watch him wipe
blood from tracks on his arm
before I leave for Palm Sunday Mass.

He swore he didn't—only pot,
which he grows in a closet.
Still. Leaving wasn't going to be easy.

We were engaged. I finally got
someone I had wanted
but the desire was dated.

Ten years ago, he was a hot
musician, in demand by bands
and a slew of gals.

Now he's a trust fund baby
in night school and I'm a
half orphaned child-woman

coming to terms with loss,
family, writing.
I want to jump off this cross.

Nineteenth and Sansom

My first love affair continued years later at the old Warwick Hotel.
Now condemned, it sits across from the Emergency Aid Building
that once housed virginal girls new to Philly; a cove still shelters
Holy Mary who protects gals roaming city streets.

On the block lies Sophy Curson, the boutique where my mother
bought pieces for her trousseau, classy clothes for the coveted
Niagara Falls honeymoon. Like mother's, my body remained intact,
but few knew we concealed continually violated souls.

Echoes of Marvin Gaye lyrics in my head, Sinatra in hers—
emboldened by pain.

Gold Mine

The geography of time
takes me back to music maps.
Before images, comments and "likes,"

I used my psyche to communicate,
especially in summer, with a beige
transistor radio tethered to my hip.

Like a secret prize in a Crackerjack box,
new songs would emerge from the
Beatles, Rolling Stones, Al Green.

I never knew what gold Marvin Gaye
would mine to move my feet and heart,
giving me the power to switch "on."

Summer Haze

Birthday parties in the breezeway.
Cousins galore gather 'round a bakery cake—
a huge swimming pool with sugary blue diving board.
She made every occasion special.

Yet again, he returns home from work bellowing.
We never learned how to tame the air.
My mother blamed his crazy clan.
Hours later, he's happily whistling about.

At thirteen, I get my first kiss in the backyard playhouse.
A threesome with the Stauffer twins;
my face assaulted by twirling tongues.
None of it ever like it played out in the old movies.

Chaste Dates

Tender green leaves of late April
remind me of chaste dates with Ray.

We retraced steps at familiar haunts through the season—
The Cloisters, Dia:Beacon, Enoteca Maria in Staten Island.

Hard to say *addio* as his smooth edges blend in.
Our ardor extinguished in May before fuchsia azaleas

caught fire. Gentle touching no longer bearable—
now used to the blazing strokes of a bass player from Brazil.

Nights belong to Joao whose passion sustains my dull days
working for the man. His music revives me, has me smiling.

No Happy Ending

I breathe in his scent,
shun his sultry gaze,
and leave the party
early and alone.

He pursues me.
I like his words, manner,
the Irish accent I hadn't caught
at first listen, the walk to the train.

Weeks later, amid silence,
his words slice through me.
Despite his younger years,
I want more than a fleeting encounter.

I'm willing to caress another raging ego.
Take on emotional havoc.
Who doesn't want to believe
this time you're the one?

Magazine Street

Leaving Lafayette Cemetery destination Guy's Po' Boys
I traipsed to the famed street lined with art and antique stores.

Too far to walk in the heat and hunger,
I stood for a bus, when he started chatting,

a fellow Pennsylvanian and music lover, in NOLA
without his late wife whom he nursed through ALS.

We both wanted to hit Ogden Museum, impressed with the idea
of self-taught artists' work on display.

But I never saw him again and in those three
Southern minutes, formed a memory.

Unfinished

At dusk, small penguins wash ashore at Phillip Island.
They hesitate, waddle forward, swish backwards

into the surf, not ready to embrace the night.
We stopped speaking, if you can call words

sent to a computer screen, on a random basis, talk.
You hide like the little animals burrowing in the sand,

free from strangers' stares and forbidden camera flashes.
I spoke to my last lover by phone. Lured him with voice.

Sound incited hearts. Words weren't shackled to a screen.
Playful, they flew on waves, bouncing from soul to soul.

Healing Poetry

At the indie bookstore's open mic, we sit
'round a table. Outside it's March Madness.

Villanova fans swarm the pike's bars.
A college student and her mother join us late.

The plain girl with long thin hair
sports glasses and an awkwardness.

She reads of a stuffed animal who served
as best friend. The loneliness that could have

choked her. Touches on a learning disability
and bullies. I was uplifted by grace

that emerged and powerful poetry,
writing that clearly saved her life.

Power in a Thumb

Back when phones were immobile
and laptops futuristic,
we possessed little money,
but owned freedom.

Minutes overflowed.
Boredom afflicted us endlessly;
we embraced it.

Planning was for bores.
When we got too big for our bikes,
in our hip huggers, midriff tops and sneakers,

we sought danger.
All we had to do was
wear a sultry scowl

and flash a thumb.
We trusted strangers to take us
anywhere we wanted to go.

LIGHT

When in Italy

Feel beautiful in Rome.
Grab a bike and get happy in Ferrara,
the planned Renaissance city
where people travel by cycle
'round ancient walls and along the Po.

Retrace Joyce's steps in Trieste,
and feel the splash of the Adriatic's far north reach.
Work hard in Milan
where serious Italians operate on Swiss time.

Greet my cousins in Teramo
where hills shrouded in gold
harbor lambs and mushrooms.

Get mystic in Ravenna
where East meets West
and Byzantine mosaics adorn
centuries' old cathedrals.

Uncover Italy's true masterpieces in Positano—
sea and sky and rock,
the big hole in the mountain

that resembles, well, anatomy,
and then indulge in heaping
plates of *spaghetti con vongole.*
Pledge to stay forever and never go back.

Retro Rider

Ducati's gone vintage and
resurrected the Scrambler,

Steve McQueen's bike of choice
as a war prisoner in *The Great Escape.*

I once rode on the back of a Harley.
Grad school at thirty had its perks.

Fearless and helmet-less, I clutched
the seat, not my odd Italian-American date,

as we whirred past cacti flanking
the Phoenix highway.

Ten years later at Ducati headquarters
as a reporter for *Advertising Age,*

I hoped for a test ride, but had to settle for a photo.
Me and Ducati. Living in the land of tortellini,

where my taste now ran to fire-engine red motorcycles
whose drivers were devastatingly handsome and spoke perfect Italian.

Venice Reveries

The bereft nightlife uplifts.
We walk beside shadows
in search of *cicchetti,*
something authentic to prolong the hush.

I forgo tourism and calves' liver.
Buy a mask and hide in Burano
island of lace, seafood, and vibrant colors.

Like Hemingway, I retreat to Torcello,
write about a river and trees.
Make a date with my muse
to meet at *Ponte del Diavolo.*

Contemplating Abruzzo

The driver tells me the English are coming.
They're buying up houses—air travel's cheaper these days.
I hide my extreme displeasure. I want to keep Abruzzo
all for myself. I don't want its secrets revealed.

My origins are rooted in a land of untamed nature,
where beech trees shaped like big cotton balls dot the
rocky mountainsides. Patches of brilliant broom sprout
along hills, by roadsides, wherever they fancy.
And Abruzzo's most famous monument, a national park,
attracts chamois, eagles, wolves, and bears,

not boisterous tourists as does Tuscany, the prissy
picture postcard of a region whose perfectly
placed trees make me think the gods went a little crazy
with their manicure kit. Where the English have flocked
for years, then joined by Americans, when writers possessing
a dim understanding of the land, seduced them with their flowery
   prose.

Will the hoards appreciate Abruzzo's hidden beauty?
The Orfento Valley cloaked in a massive shadow or spotted
bright green when the sun plays hide and seek?
Medieval churches adorned with little gold and ancient
abbeys situated off the beaten track? Will they savor lamb stew,
pasta shaped like guitar strings, and pork roasted to perfection?
The traffic is bad enough as is, even in the smallest city.

I want to put a reserved sign on Abruzzo's pristine beaches.
I still remember the striped hues of the Adriatic and the pale
green surf that popped into view shortly after the train left Pescara.
Mellow waves, mimicking teasing tongues, shot up every which way.

Festa Della Donna

Today vendors on every corner of Milan will gift
brilliant mimosas to ladies passing by—
female friends will dine in *trattorie* without their beaus.
Some traditions stay etched on your soul.

A friend in Hove will celebrate her mother's birthday,
lay a ring of flowers at her Brighton grave.
The once vibrant school principal spent
final years in her daughter's care. I was there.

Two gallant gals working as stringers in Italy
embraced a future full of new beginnings and fun.
They met fulfillment in unexpected ways, found love
where it all began, clutching yellow dreams on Ladies' Day.

Yellow

The day after fashion designer Gianni Versace
was found murdered in Miami,

I rushed to the thrift shop on Milan's Via Cavour
to retrieve the bright yellow cashmere jacket

I had consigned. I wanted to keep a memento
of Versace's talent, of my fleeting fling with fashion.

Today when I wear that jacket on the streets
of Manhattan people wave and yell out.

It makes them smile.

Men of the Cloth

They wield needles, tapelines and scissors,
use fine fabric canvases to fashion suits of gold.
Transform everyday people into figures of position.

Three proud Italians with creative temperaments
and a passion to share their endangered skills.
Joseph Centofanti, who survived five years

as a British prisoner of war in Kenya, brought his passion
to Ardmore, Pennsylvania. At 90, he trains a young apprentice
who longs to be part of this fading tradition.

Nino Corvato left Sicily to ply a profession whose training
began at age seven. He aces his career with a Brooks Brothers
stint before flying solo and opening an atelier on Madison Avenue.

Checchino Fonticoli stays home in Abruzzo's Penne,
gives tailoring a modern twist at Brioni where old world meets
new world production and a school for tomorrow's tailors thrives.

All three cater to clients who shun throwaway
chic for fit, buy beautiful clothes with interiors to match,
from masters of the cloth yet to be replaced by factories.

SOUNDS

Master Plan

Square white goatee and
long blue tunic swinging,

"Pharoah" Sanders prances on stage,
wishing us peace and love.

He reverently clasps his horn
and serenades a packed house at Birdland.

No Twitter handles at play,
Tony Hewitt sings about

going steady, takes us all
back to a gentler time.

Musicians throng the space, eyes and
ears attuned to Sanders, who in his
seventy-fifth year, is ablaze.

Clifford Plays Somethin'

I want to live my life like
Clifford plays the drums.
Coolly observing the heady scene,

he has a feathery touch.
Sits behind a glittery rust-hued set of skins,
still body, head held high.

Brushing the drums on "Caravan,"
orchestrating the rhythm on each tune,
wowing the crowd on a solo.

Face masking emotion,
but hands and arms energized.
Goes easy on the exhale.

Wearing his black beret straight up,
accented by a crisp, tangerine shirt
at Somethin' Jazz club—a laid-back lair on East 52nd.

So unexpected it's beyond chill.
Like Clifford, who steals a gaze at the crowd
before returning his focus to work.

Music Lessons

Dressed in a short summer frock and matching bloomers,
she starts piano lessons at four, plays scales for Miss Geiger,
an old maid ensconced in a stone cottage across the street,
who slaps her when she hits a wrong key.
For the next ten years, she continues her studies
at the local conservatory, run by a highbrow uncle and
his opera-singing wife. She sits in a stiff chair
in a room off the porch of the Victorian house
and waits to be summoned for the half-hour one-on-one.
A new teacher each year, but none can foster a passion.
She prefers to sway to the sweet ballads of Al Green,
listen for favorite hits on her radio or play the new
Carly Simon record. So she locks herself away
in the big bedroom with her father's stereo and
contemplates the lyrics and wishes for time to pass
fast, so she, too, can experience anticipation.
Fast forward fifteen years. She only has time for elusive
musicians like Dan, who lays aside his bass and joins her
on the bed, plays her lithe body as if it were a rare guitar
as he peels away the layers of waiting. Now she understands
the music, revels in it, prefers this position, the role of muse.

Romance Chelsea Style

We met in our apartment building.
Once I saw the sheathed guitar,
I prayed he wasn't gay.

Then he kissed me on the subway
after our first date at Maxwell's.
He kept a pad and pen in his pocket,

an appendage to his heart.
He spoke to me in melody,
buried questions in verse.

He turned me on to songwriters he idolized—
Robyn Hitchcock, Juliana Hatfield, Jane Siberry.
On my birthday he gave me a gift that will last forever,

a nameless song that called me the brightest star.
It took years to wean myself off him,
much longer than it took him to quit the needle.

Live at Noon

With her shock of white hair
and skeletal demeanor,

St. Vincent commandeered the guitar.
Her powerful voice beguiled the mix

of hippies and hipsters who gravitate
to the World Café for free music

Fridays at noon. I came for the company,
a long-ago friend who once shared

adventures in musicians before I conquered
Italy and fashion glossies. And she stayed
close to home to breed kids and divorces.

Visions

The night of the Steven Wilson concert,
I awoke every twenty minutes haunted
by visions—a man's face locked in a frame.

Was it the prog rock singer of Porcupine Tree fame?
I had joined zealots of his 'poetry of melancholy'
at the sold-out Beacon Theatre gig. They were

heading to Chicago for the next show. A neophyte,
I listened and watched his performance in awe.
Massive video art as backdrop with everyday

London scenes starring a sultry brunette, the desert,
shades of yellow and purple. Singer Ninet Tayeb
joined him onstage as he drank tea to combat a cold.

The night ended with their duo of Bowie's "Space Oddity"
as a striking headshot of the late prophet lit up the stage.

Understanding Jaco

That one song still holds the power to haunt.
I peeled apart its soulful layers searching for

the truth or an obscure meaning, as if trying to
conjure up the face of a loved one long gone.

An ode to an intangible is what captivated me.
I replayed the melody and saw your hands fondling

the bass at that South Street club, like fresh thoughts
of trysts with an old love interest who once rocked your world.

But I went back to a time when the demons began to tantalize you.
I wanted to understand such a confusing and elusive song.

Like you, the bass-playing wonder who after years of saying
"no" turned to "yeses" that paved your undoing.

As you traveled down dark streets and indiscriminately
picked your battles, you abandoned reason and the roles

of leader, teacher, friend and muse.
I now listen to "Three Views of a Secret" for its pure beauty,

as if wandering through a magnificent art gallery and
ignoring the placards. An anthem from a legend who couldn't

shield himself from the music world's harsher angles.
A brilliant legacy. But you left the stage too soon.

Swinging Jazz

(Inspired by the late bass player Victor Bailey)

A steamy July set the mood for jazz.
Victor Bailey's putting on a party
to tape music he adores.

Dropping our Manhattan cool, we give in to
Brooklyn's pull—air and space, Shapeshifter Lab's
wide white room, walls splashed
with vibrant murals of musicians at play.

Fans and friends jive to a booming bass.
Drummer Lenny White carries the beat.
Alex Foster's horn seduces.
Mino Cinelu on percussion creates magical sounds.

Sweet guitar licks fill the night.
A flirting filmmaker records the show.
We salute the moment with Spanish white.
Victor basks in rhythm and swing,

inspires and energizes. A sapping illness lurks,
but Victor's faith and funk drive his spirit.
A spontaneous family formed.
Ready to dance again.

Bahia Beats

Percussionist Davi Vieira speaks all languages
in the tongue of drums, triangle, jazzy castanets,
a set of bells that hangs from his mic.

He seduces fans with his thumping hands.
We respond to his Bahia beats
with hips and feet.

Can't hide the heat.
Swaying to his fast *forro*
strains from Northeast Brazil.

Sundays at 9 at Club Bonafide on East 52nd Street.
Fellow Brazilians on guitar, bass,
fiery red Yamaha drums.

Blame it on Salvador, home of Davi,
storyteller Jorge Amado, and
Africans who hit the shores in the 1500s,

where the Atlantic's thrashing waves are wildest.
He sings "Caipirinha" and I could order another
but the music gets me plenty high.

Dancing to samba.
Serenaded by songs and laughter and his bright smile.
The best moves all down below.

Luisa plays on a Flying V violin,
swings like she never has before.
Davi can't hide his joy at

tantalizing fans wrapped in a trance,
like worshippers of Candomblé, the religion of Brazil.
Capped with a checkered green hat, he prances on stage.

The club manager takes to the floor.
Midnight strikes too soon.

Bop Juice

I arrived at Small's Jazz early to find a long line outside.
So fine to see fans in their 20s and 30s.
Got the best seat in the house, atop the short bar.

Clifford hides under a green checkered cap,
behind a sporty sweater striped yellow.
So smooth from the onset.
No banging on his sizzling drums.

He's got the intricate beat down,
tap, tap, tap.
Tippity tap.
Band leader Ralph LaLamma blows his horn.

David Wong stands upright at the bass.
Gershwin, "Antiqua," "Love Letters."
"Love Walked In"—
the last book my mother gave me
inspired by the obscure standard.

Like good loving—the music's slow,
lively. It's all the juice I need tonight.

HOME

Soundtrack to My Mother's Life

She loved to croon especially when sad.
"Smile," whose music Charlie Chaplin wrote,
remained an all-time favorite.

Another personal hit, "My Funny Valentine,"
I found sad until I discovered jazz and Chet Baker.
She deserved a better shot at love.

But she romanced life, found beauty elsewhere.
"The Shadow of Your Smile," so appropriate,
as her smile sparkled. It follows me everywhere.

City on a River

What Chester made no longer makes Chester.
Scott Paper, Ford Motor Company left for sunnier climes.
Blight replaced a factory town flanked by a shipyard
and ethnic neighborhoods that glowed.

Before communities dismantled and racial clamor tolled,
mapping out his peace plan, Martin Luther King chose the city
for divinity studies at Crozer Seminary.

Landmarks of learning endure, like Pennsylvania Military College
now Widener University, and Chester High School.
I pore over my mother's yellowed letters.

Chester High students credit their old English teacher
for love of reading, guidance, success.
I feel a flicker of her hometown allure.
Change rains lightly.

A national soccer team built a stadium in the city's largest park.
Games sell out.
Freighters glide by.
The glistening Delaware River reflects the stars.

Amelia

A lady from Puglia landed
in East Harlem in the early 1900s.
She bore eight children, including my father.

Headed by an unskilled laborer,
the family relocated to Bryn Mawr.
I hear my grandmother held court

from a fluffy sofa
next to a living room staircase.
She insisted her children see no hurdles,

emulate the prosperous WASPs
who settled on Philadelphia's Main Line.
I hear she taught Italian immigrants English.

I hear she served tea from a real silver service
to *paesani* who visited her tiny row home.
I hear she pilfered a close friend's sweater.

My father adored her.
My mother said she was crazy.
I bear her name and want to be
nothing and everything like her.

A Bridge to Antonio

My lone recollection is visiting you
at Lankenau Hospital, as a curious
four-year-old granddaughter.

You, in a post-stroke state. A mop of white hair
and round wire-rimmed glasses framed
your fragile smile. For years, my father

wondered "what went through your head"
as you trudged home from a laborer's
job to a family of eight kids, tucked into

a three-bedroom row home. I hear you
carried debts when you courted
my grandmother, and feared her ire.

I learned you loved to joke with friends,
that you helped build the Brooklyn Bridge,
a landmark in the city where we both landed.

Soundtrack to My Father's Life

He loved Gershwin, big bands, opera, marching bands.
My father studied violin at the Bryn Mawr Conservatory
of Music, a school started by his oldest brother, a lofty ambition
for the son of Italian immigrants and one of eight children.

The house felt barren after he left.
Music no longer sprang from corners of rooms.
I remember his favorites—"Yellow Bird,"
"Mood Indigo," "Bye-Bye Blackbird."

I salvaged his vinyl collection from the basement, making space
above ground for his 45s from Decca Records, a 78
of Liberace's "Dark Eyes," a Bing Crosby tune "When the Moon
Comes Over Madison Square." Today I live near the park.

Paper Boy's Daughter

The crumpling of newspapers still echoes.
My father reading the *Philadelphia Inquirer*
with morning coffee. Flipping pages of the

Evening Bulletin before dozing in his chair.
Only seven, he rose at five a.m. to deliver papers.
Honored work from then on.

His hardware store staff enjoyed two daily papers
on the half-hour lunch break.
The town news agency, once abuzz with traffic,

now sits off the pike's center.
Alone in the store, I search for a recent byline,
still revere the printed page and worlds it opens.

Echoes of a Hardware Store

His strong hands endured life's stages.
They're all I recognized on the day of final goodbyes.

With fingertips slightly callused, he didn't have the hands
of a doctor or a lawyer or a corporate dad.
They were the hands of a hardware store merchant.

Such a bygone expression, but one I glimpsed on countless
old documents, as I took inventory of his material world.

He mastered the nuts and bolts of life: make lists,
pray before bed, be loyal to family, spend less than you earn.

He wasn't mechanical or a fixer-upper, but good with money,
more of a dreamer and childlike in his simplicity.

The massive storefront celebrated the seasons.
Gleaming red barbeque grills and green webbed lawn chairs in summer,

twinkling Christmas displays and brass fireplace sets in winter,
fertilizer in spring and rakes in fall.

We played with reverence in his workplace, listened for his fast gait,
which a monstrous illness eventually lassoed.

Traditions ebb; simple joys lose poignancy.
But cherished memories spring up

when I walk the freshly-oiled floors
of an old-fashioned hardware store.

Travels with You

You accompany me on my travels,
share the joy that infects me
when I explore a place for the first time.

Whether home or in distant lands,
I feel you holding out a hand,
indicating where to stop next as I drift.

Thank you for the gift of wonder,
for raising me with the zest for discovery,
for instilling me with the grit to journey alone.

You taught us not to fear life,
but to grab it, inhale it, run to adventures.
Maybe you weren't the bad parent after all.

Fall in Philadelphia

Days burst with time.
Leaves aflame with color.
We trudged through neat piles
toward grownup-hood.
We had all that we wanted.

Youth untouched by earthquakes and aftershocks,
we found shelter from the autumn chill
playing touch football with neighbors.
Unaware we wanted for nothing.

This morning an oil painting beckons—
a gazebo strewn with wispy vines and
landscape of pink blossoms—
draws me to dream, backward and forward.
We want all that we had.

Views from the Driveway

A small stretch of space afforded a window on the world,
the promise of escape from harmful clutches that lurked inside.
Freedom is a bicycle in red or turquoise or deep purple.
Grasping banana-shaped handlebars, one circled toward independence.
Mastered the initial phases of love-making with neighbors, friends,
    passersby.

On steamy, sultry days, the surface shot off a pungent perfume.
Mixing with the sun's scent on young skin and nubile grass clippings.
Summer in the suburbs had arrived. Butterfly days called for loose
    plans
and clandestine trips to the private duck pond
to roll down grassy hills and puff on stolen cigarettes.

Time answered most important questions.
And in the Europe of my mind—
breezeways are still in vogue,
families seek shade beneath Kelly green awnings,
girls dare to draw the sun with aluminum foil.
We still marvel at the sight of fireflies come dusk.

At the Bird Sanctuary

A comforting stillness,
tropical-like greens form an oasis of shade.
Spurts of daffodils blanket the floor of this secret room
where reveries of another time haunt.

When in the throes of panic fourteen years ago,
I discovered the mini-park
and from a bench sought solace.

Prayed for nature to take its course;
I couldn't imagine life with an aimless musician,
preferred the path of travel and youth that few strings prolongs.

I now return to pray that nature reverse its course,
for a vitality to return to my mother that the stroke robbed,
that she relearn to speak, read, write, drive.

Half-hurriedly, I pass the verdant haven longing to stay.
Priorities sit on a constantly revolving Lazy Susan.
I didn't realize I had the perfect life.

Roles reordered, I rush off to an aging parent,
to cook, clean, and shop in an overly-bright suburban supermarket.
I long for conversation that will never come.

I watch her watch TV.
She shuffles to the kitchen for the highlight of her day:
three hearty meals, always dessert.
And I thought I'd never be able to make up for all the dinners she
    cooked.

Last Words

She spoke her last words
to me the night of her stroke
when I had no idea

that morning wouldn't come.
For four years
dark days of juggling

work and caregiving,
legal battles with siblings.
Then I heard her

call out my name in a hushed tone,
as I was leaving to say goodbye
the day of her burial.

Remembered Dreams

I hold a baby in my arms and cry.
Is she mine?

Delivering Meals on Wheels to seniors,
my hot musician boyfriend by my side.

I visit a friend in Florence and get a
late night call, "Dad died."

Blank Page

Words won't come.
Had little to say today,
yesterday, last month.

Do muses take vacations?
If so, I hope she's in Malta
or Montana or Pittsburgh—

places on the bucket list that grows shorter.
Why couldn't I write about the Asian woman
in purple rubber boots at the Chelsea station,

loudly asking the guy with earbuds for directions
or the red fox in my dreams that lives in the fields
that flank my friend's farmhouse

or the wounds that never healed from that day
in fifth grade when I went to school covered in welts?

Secrets

I didn't know my mother loved pink roses
until the day I ordered floral arrangements for her funeral Mass.
She didn't seem to care much for flowers as a young mother.
She never received flowers from my father
who tended our rose gardens each summer.

I thought she considered bouquets a frivolous purchase.
Maybe she thought flowers flourished best in their natural habitat.
My mother grew up with a father whose passion was gardening.
Flowers, most of whose names I never learned,
framed the backdrop of my childhood summers.

But pink roses? I had to discover an intimate slice
of my mother's life from a neighborhood store owner?
I recall the woman at the florist exclaiming,
"Oh yes, she always asked for pink roses when ordering
flowers for anniversaries and birthdays."

Pink roses do resemble my mother—
subtle, sweet flowers from the regal rose family.
She once gave me a stunning oil painting
when I moved to a new apartment in New York,

excitedly took it from her bedroom wall
and presented my only housewarming gift.
I've looked at that artwork every morning for five years,
and only now realize the perky flowers in the silver bowl are pink
    roses.

She left us one overcast morning in late September.
She was weak,
no longer brimming with joy for life,
after confined to her home for too long.

I took all her worldly possessions for granted,
so many of them remnants of our life back
in our only house on Pennsylvania Avenue.

Only now I see pink roses on the Limoges vanity set,
pink roses on a German vase in the powder room,
pink roses on the edges of a condiment holder,
pink roses on a nick-less decorative plate.

On Memorial Day, as I crossed West Side Highway
    to get to the gym,
I was met by bush upon bush of pink roses
    that danced in the breeze.
On my last birthday, a close friend sent me the first card
    of the special day—
sparkles outlined large petals of pink roses.

I now believe my mother speaks to me in pink roses;
what else did she love that I don't know?

Protected

Captured in black and white circa 1948.
A bust shot of my mother with her much younger sister.

Porcelain skin.
Deep-colored mouths.

Dark, clear eyes.
The sheen of black virgin hair.

Gazes in unison.
Wearing high-necked dresses.
A halo of light atop their heads.

Two adult cherubs, workforce pioneers:
an English professor and dental hygienist.

Memorialized in a green Italian wooden frame.
Still protected.

BREEZE

Recollection

Low maintenance babies that don't cry—
brunettes and blondes with flawless faces,
cherubs forever young,
more valuable boxed than not.

An elegant madam in a flowing emerald gown,
figurines from far-off lands I've never crossed,
Portuguese maidens in vibrant swirling skirts have mouths
    that form "o,"
a Flamenco dancer in yellow satin in a voluptuous twist.

Long into adulthood, I was still drawn to them—
new and used, infants and ladies.
My sisters married and spawned.
I stuck with dolls.

Likenesses of immortal characters graced my childhood bed:
Scarlett O'Hara, the Little Women, and Maria from the
    Sound of Music.
Collectors can have their art, cars, stamps and coins.

I had model students for a classroom,
plentiful patients for a hospital,
friends who never divulged secrets,
playmates who didn't argue.

Friends joke they'll one day finance my retirement,
but I purge the idea of cashing in on
snapshots of Merry Christmases, hope for a family, forever
    companions.

I still peer into toy stores,
arrested by the sight of a dazzling doll,
curse eBay for cheapening their worth,
wonder who will inherit my treasures.

Natural Blonde

Distinguished by royal Spanish blood,
brown eyes, and white highlights,
her pedigree demands that her hair gleam

like a freshly minted gold coin.
She stands apart from the pack,
graces ancient oriental paintings,

lends pageantry to parades.
Distant cousin to Pegasus, Trigger, Mr. Ed,
the Palomino's ancestors befriended Native Americans.
Together they helped settle the new frontier.

Dream of March 14, 2003

My cousin and his partner invite me to their new home.
They tell me it's a "flage" that cost one million dollars.

Astonished that they'd leave the city,
I arrive at a townhouse development in the suburbs.

On the front lawn, a white horse in a sequin hat flounces on
   its hind legs.
I find my boyfriend Jim in the driveway,

dressed in short shorts, high heels and eyeliner.
He doesn't look half bad.

The next morning, I blame my synthetic comforter
for the night sweats and palpitations.

Dreamscapes

Blurred distances
Haunted by once familiar places.
New York has become a maze I can no longer navigate.
Rome is now a short train ride away.

Distorted time
People, long forgotten, play poignant roles on this stage.
They are integral to the stories,
more familiar than they ever were before.
I wonder why I never saw them in this light.

Fleeting encounters
The unexpected is a tonic.
It melts away the mundane elements of recent memories.
Exhilarated, I long to stay.

Altered state
I pledge to return and continue the drama,
of love gone right and travels around the world,
unplanned, baggage-free, weightless.

Lessons Learned from Moths

I learned the art of detachment
from a destructive pest
romanticized by poets
whose origins go back millions of years.

Celestial nomads that feast on
leather, wool, silk, felt
and thrive on night
taught me to let go of longing—

animals stuffed with memories,
dolls from a distant dad,
an embroidered coat from Gimbels.
When I returned to my late mother's home,

white larvae covered elegant outfits.
Soles fell from Ferragamo pumps.
Moths cunningly coached me to occupy now,
not dwell in closets lined with past lives

nor focus on nostalgia
tarnished by death and deceit.

Happy at Art

"Hopeful" and "Getting Ready to Get Down,"
I want to find joy in poetry
like Josh Ritter serenades fans.

"Homecoming" and "Kathleen."
Heart and soul smiling, he's jumping,
doing a jig as he sings,

elated to be on stage with his Royal City Band.
Energy grows "Where the Night Goes" and
no one wants the show to stop.

I want to put an end to "The Curse" of blank pages.
Need to be inspired by places and faces, put on
a "Bright Smile," take up a pen or sit at the screen
and "Baby That's Not All."

Poet Painting

Poets don't live in black and white.
We capture nature's power.
Brandishing words, I paint emerald
and topaz trees. Inject sienna into
Mediterranean memories of Italy's
Ligurian Coast in June. I revive lost fun—
digging for shells or hiding out in a secret
garden of purple hyacinths. I hear green
in summer's sounds. I recall a red rose
my mother places on a Lazy Susan
as my father's car pulls into the driveway.
I sketch the earth's perfume
as a sultry season wanes—snapping air,
mellowing light, before leaves turn brilliant.

Glad

In the pursuit,
loosen chains.

Sleep next to a dreamcatcher.
Live in places smaller than large.

Travel nearer than far.
Reach for yellow leaves that turn red in October.

Listen to classic soul, not rap.
Wear silver and turquoise jewelry, if you must.

Speak an alluring language.
Memorable encounters start with a tongue.

Fashion Monk

He fled the Spanish Civil War
to pioneer the chainmail miniskirt,
throwaway chic, the "Unwearables."

Paco Rabanne crafted dresses
from metal rings, paper, and plastic.
He concocted citrusy perfumes
and Barbarella's space-age costumes.

Now free, he travels non-stop in search
of his place in the cosmos. He sees auras.
Rejects the fluff his customers covet.

Fashioned a Spartan life free of attachment.
Blames technology for the fear
and stress gripping planet Earth.

Orange Is My New Black

I'm tossing black from my world—
black clothes, black cars, black moods.
Banishing dread and gloom.

Black was cool at sixteen and slimming at thirty.
Now I'm occupying orange-hued vibes,
loosening the shackles to dark tones.

I'm deporting colorless lingerie and sex.
When I sleep, instead of jumping into black puddles,
I'm going to emerge from tangerine dreams. Glowing.

End of the Road

When the open road beckoned,
we connected with the land,
at a teepee flanked by the Rio Grande

or a picnic spot with slanted roof, fringed
by Monument Valley's orange mountains.
Landmarks for memories, roadside rest stops

opened windows onto cultures.
The middle of the road vibrated with color.
We relished time eating slow food or getting lost

in a vista. As the journey ends for these highway icons,
I salute the red, white and blue hangar in Flower Mound, Texas
where travelers, not airplanes, made a last stop.

Night Revelations

Best confessions take place in the dark—
professing love during an ardent tryst,

sharing fantasies with a new lover
at the Madonna Inn,

priestly chats that sear sin.
Nocturnal visits from friends once trusted

—so much safer to cherish them in dreams.
Making self-vows that it's never going to happen again.

And if I can, I hope to take the Reaper's hand during sleep,
when golden light breaks darkness.

We Became Summer

Long before we needed protection,
we formed tribes and picked a chief.
First-borns have a knack for stirring idolatry.

Bike rides energized us on innocent mornings.
The sun perfumed our fresh skin,
before self-awareness replaced laughter
and possession replaced play.

At dusk, seduction set in.
Bruises faded and mosquitoes fled.
Lightning bugs appeared, as beer-soaked dads

threw teen neighbors into backyard swimming pools
and we invited boys into the playhouse shed,
before ennui replaced embracing fear of the unknown.

CPSIA information can be obtained
at www.ICGtesting.com
Printed in the USA
BVHW071952151118
533238BV00001B/20/P

9 781630 450533